BODY SYSTEMS

The Circulatory System

by Kay Manolis

Consultant:
Molly Martin, M.D.
Internal Medicine
MeritCare, Bemidji, MN

BELLWETHER MEDIA • MINNEAPOLIS, MN

J 612.1
Manolis

Note to Librarians, Teachers, and Parents:

Blastoff! Readers are carefully developed by literacy experts and combine standards-based content with developmentally appropriate text.

Level 1 provides the most support through repetition of high-frequency words, light text, predictable sentence patterns, and strong visual support.

Level 2 offers early readers a bit more challenge through varied simple sentences, increased text load, and less repetition of high-frequency words.

Level 3 advances early-fluent readers toward fluency through increased text and concept load, less reliance on visuals, longer sentences, and more literary language.

Level 4 builds reading stamina by providing more text per page, increased use of punctuation, greater variation in sentence patterns, and increasingly challenging vocabulary.

Level 5 encourages children to move from "learning to read" to "reading to learn" by providing even more text, varied writing styles, and less familiar topics.

Whichever book is right for your reader, Blastoff! Readers are the perfect books to build confidence and encourage a love of reading that will last a lifetime!

This edition first published in 2009 by Bellwether Media, Inc.

No part of this publication may be reproduced in whole or in part without written permission of the publisher. For information regarding permission, write to Bellwether Media, Inc., Attention: Permissions Department, Post Office Box 19349, Minneapolis, MN 55419.

Library of Congress Cataloging-in-Publication Data
Manolis, Kay.
  Circulatory system / by Kay Manolis.
    p. cm. – (Blastoff! readers: body systems)
  Includes bibliographical references and index.
  Summary: "Introductory text explains the functions and physical concepts of the circulatory system with color photography and simple scientific diagrams. Intended for students in grades three through six"–Provided by publisher.
  ISBN-13: 978-1-60014-242-0 (hardcover : alk. paper)
  ISBN-10: 1-60014-242-7 (hardcover : alk. paper)
  1. Cardiovascular system–Juvenile literature. I. Title.
  QP103.M25 2009
  612.1–dc22   2008032693

Contents

What Is the Circulatory System? 4

Your Heart   6

Your Blood   8

Your Blood Vessels   16

A Healthy Circulatory System   18

Glossary   22

To Learn More   23

Index   24

What Is the Circulatory System?

Can you feel your heart pound after a fast run? Your heart works hard when you exercise. It also works when you rest.

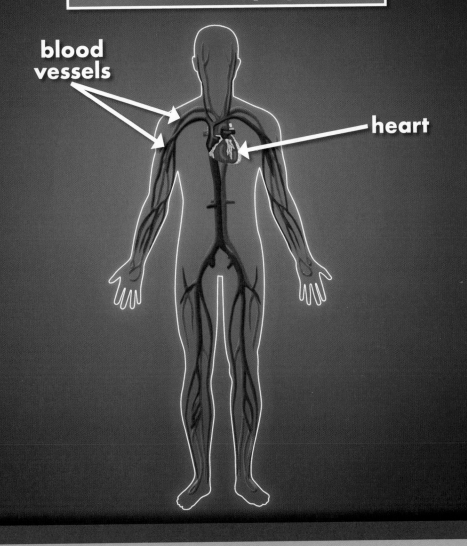

The Circulatory System

blood vessels

heart

The movements of your heart keep blood moving through your body. Your heart pumps blood through tubes called **blood vessels**. Your heart, blood, and blood vessels make up your circulatory system.

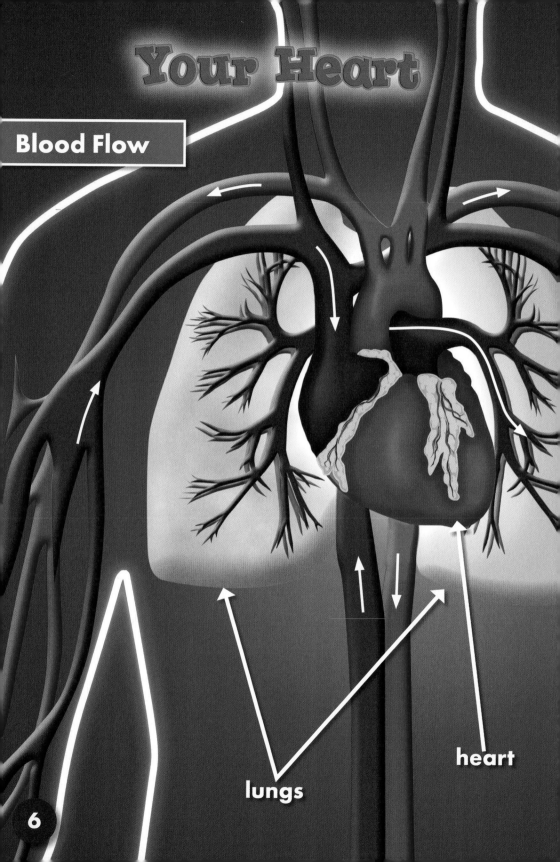

Blood Flow

lungs

heart

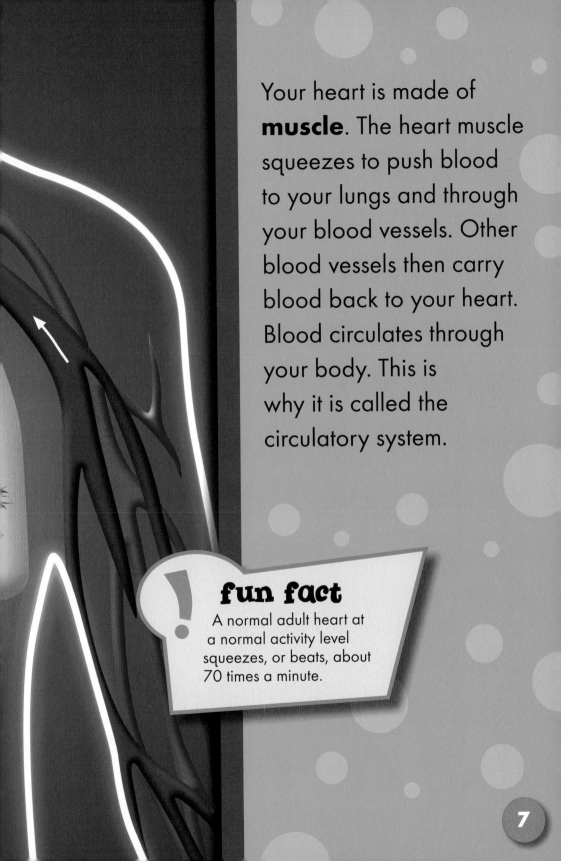

Your heart is made of **muscle**. The heart muscle squeezes to push blood to your lungs and through your blood vessels. Other blood vessels then carry blood back to your heart. Blood circulates through your body. This is why it is called the circulatory system.

fun fact

A normal adult heart at a normal activity level squeezes, or beats, about 70 times a minute.

Your Blood

Blood does important work for your body. Blood contains many kinds of **cells**. One kind of cell is called a **platelet**. These help blood **clot** if you get cut. Platelets clump together and harden to stop blood from flowing. If clots did not form, all of your blood could flow out of a cut!

! fun fact
One drop of blood contains about 250,000 platelets.

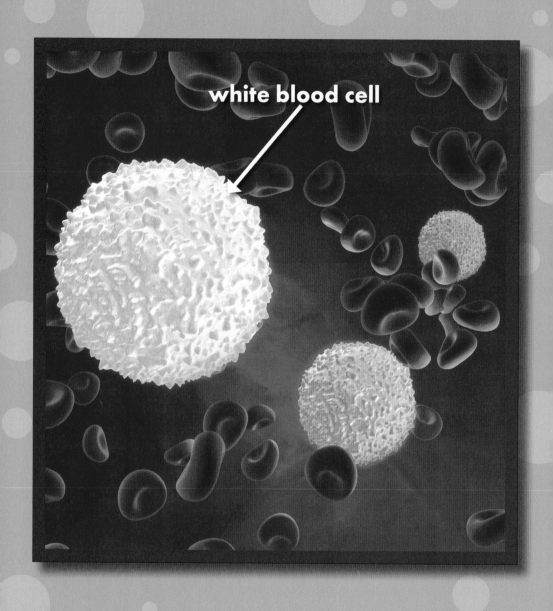

white blood cell

White blood cells in your blood help keep you healthy. **Viruses** and **bacteria** can enter your blood and make you sick.

White blood cells can destroy these invaders.
This can keep you from getting sick. If you
do get sick, your white blood cells help
you get well.

Blood also has **red blood cells**. These carry **oxygen** to all of the other cells in your body.

Your body is made up of billions of cells. You have skin cells, bone cells, and many other kinds of cells. Each cell needs oxygen to survive.

fun fact

Blood can travel up to 10 miles (16 kilometers) per hour. When the body is at rest, it takes only about 8 seconds for blood to go from the heart to the brain and back again.

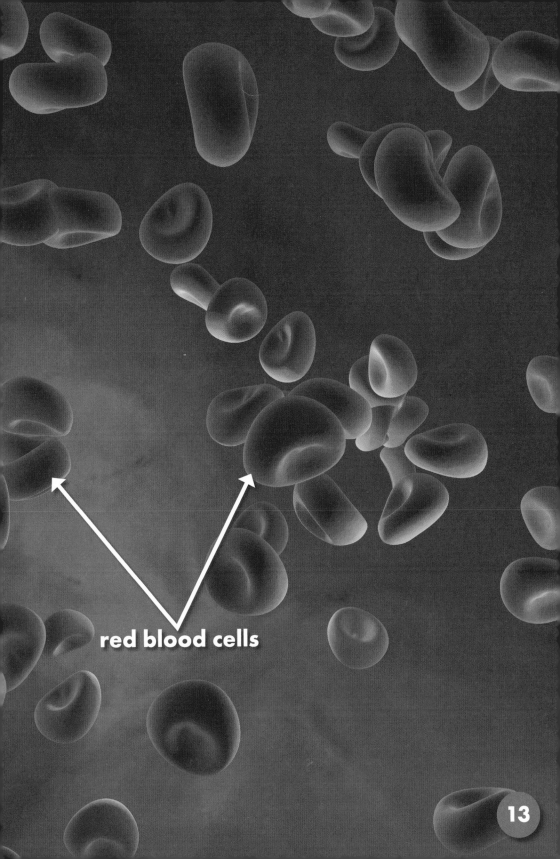

red blood cells

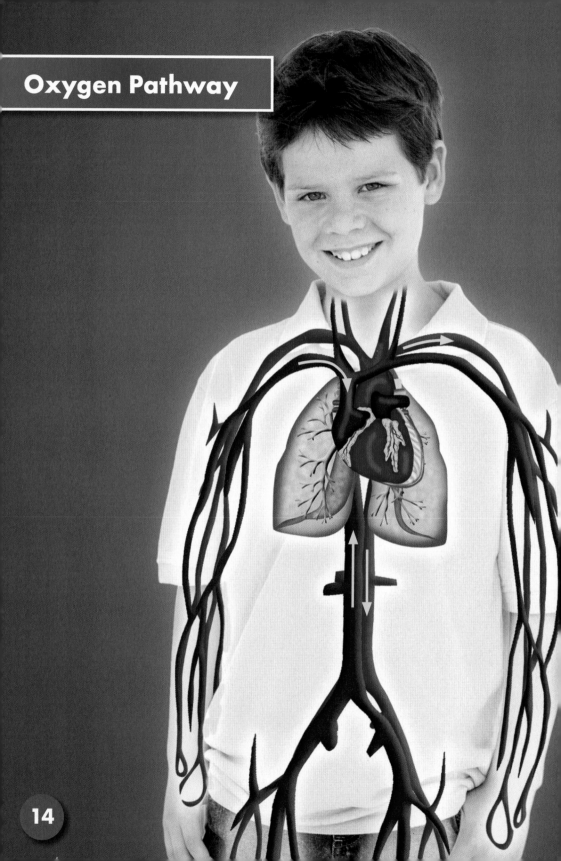

The oxygen in your blood comes from air. You bring air into your lungs when you breathe. Oxygen from the air mixes with your blood. Your heart pumps the oxygen-filled blood to the rest of your body. Your cells take the oxygen from the blood. **Carbon dioxide** leaves cells and moves into blood. Blood carrying carbon dioxide flows back to your heart. The blood is then pumped back to your lungs. Then you breathe out the carbon dioxide.

RED=blood carrying oxygen

BLUE=blood carrying carbon dioxide

Your Blood Vessels

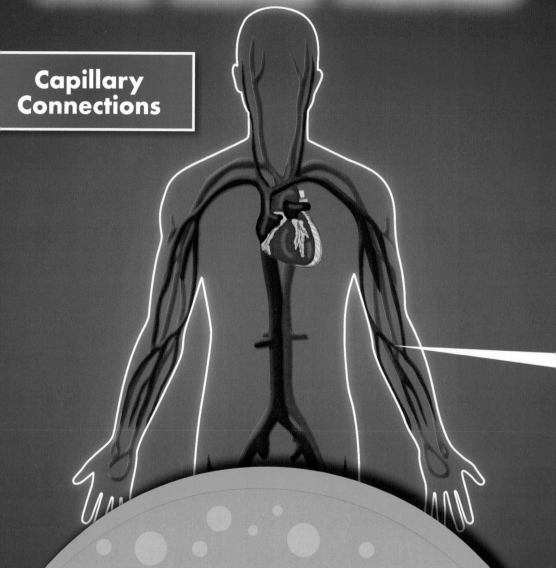

Blood vessels run through every part of your body. **Arteries** are vessels that carry blood away from the heart to the rest of the body. **Veins** carry blood back to the heart.

Capillaries are the smallest blood vessels. They connect arteries and veins. Inside capillaries, oxygen moves out of blood into cells. Carbon dioxide from the cells moves into blood to be carried away.

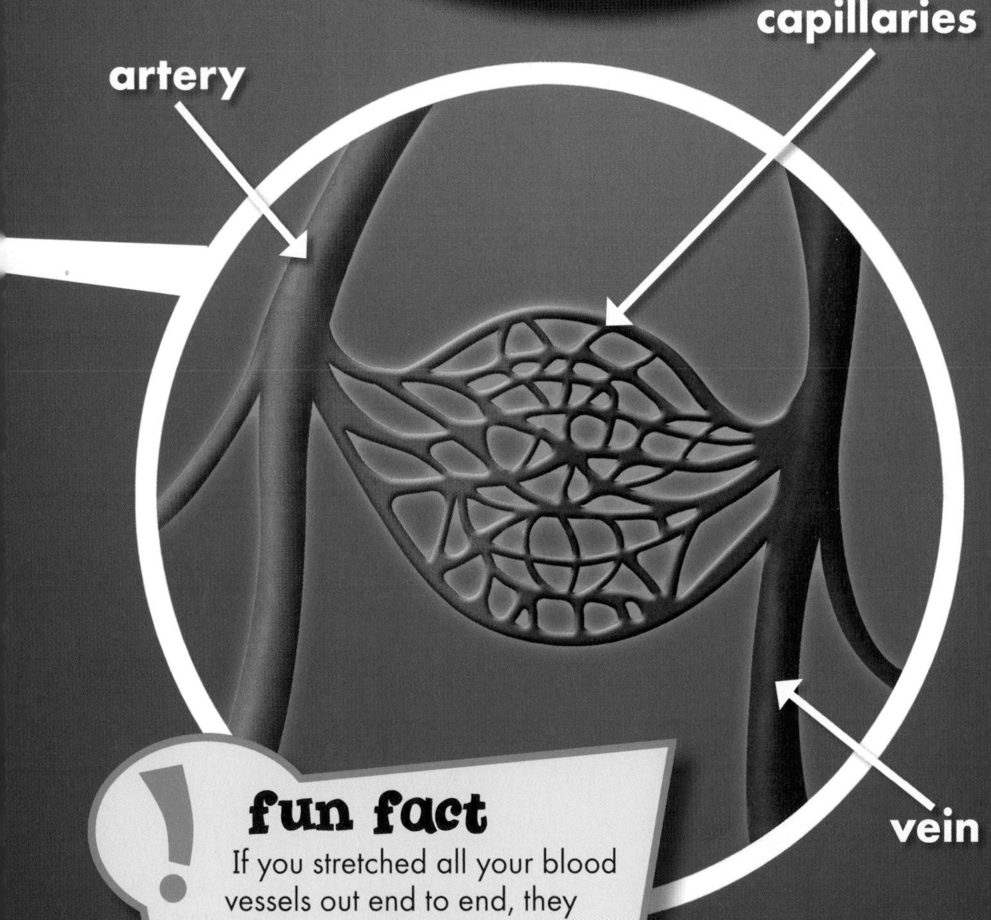

capillaries

artery

vein

fun fact
If you stretched all your blood vessels out end to end, they would be over 62,000 miles (100,000 kilometers) long.

A Healthy Circulatory System

Exercise helps keep your circulatory system healthy. Your muscle cells need extra oxygen when they work hard.

Your heart beats faster to pump more blood to your muscles. This extra work makes your heart stronger.

Eating healthy foods is also good for your circulatory system. Choose fresh fruits and vegetables every day. Think about all the work your circulatory system does for you. Do your best to keep it healthy!

Glossary

arteries—blood vessels that carry blood from the heart to other parts of the body

bacteria—tiny living things made of just one cell; some bacteria can cause disease while others help your body.

blood vessels—strong tubes that carry blood throughout the body

capillaries—the tiniest blood vessels that connect arteries to veins

carbon dioxide—a waste material released by human cells; your blood carries carbon dioxide to your lungs and you breathe it out.

cells—the basic building blocks of living things

clot—to clump together and harden

muscle—a body part that can squeeze and produce force or motion

oxygen—a gas in air that human cells need to stay alive; you breathe in oxygen and your blood carries it to your cells.

platelets—tiny cells in blood that form clots when there is an injury to a blood vessel

red blood cells—parts of blood that carry oxygen to all the cells of the body

veins—blood vessels that carry blood back to the heart

viruses—tiny things that can cause disease; viruses can only grow inside living cells.

white blood cells—parts of blood that fight disease

To Learn More

AT THE LIBRARY
Green, Emily K. *Keeping Fit*. Minneapolis, Minn.: Bellwether, 2007.

Simon, Seymour. *The Heart: Our Circulatory System.* New York: HarperCollins, 2006.

Taylor-Butler, Christine. *The Circulatory System*. New York: Children's Press, 2008.

ON THE WEB
Learning more about the circulatory system is as easy as 1, 2, 3.

1. Go to www.factsurfer.com.

2. Enter "circulatory system" into the search box.

3. Click the "Surf" button and you will see a list of related Web sites.

With factsurfer.com, finding more information is just a click away.

Index

air, 15

arteries, 16, 17

bacteria, 10

blood, 5, 7, 9, 10, 12, 15, 16, 17, 19

blood vessels, 5, 7, 16, 17

body, 5, 7, 9, 12, 15, 16

brain, 12

breathing, 15

capillaries, 17

carbon dioxide, 15, 17

cells, 9, 12, 15, 17, 18

clotting, 9

exercise, 4, 18

food, 21

heart, 4, 5, 7, 12, 15, 16, 19

lungs, 7, 15

muscle, 7, 18, 19

oxygen, 12, 15, 17, 18

platelets, 9

red blood cells, 12

rest, 4, 12

veins, 16, 17

viruses, 10

white blood cells, 10, 11

The images in this book are reproduced through the courtesy of: Sebastian Kaulitzki, front cover, pp. 10, 13; Monkey Business Images, pp. 4, 14; Linda Clavel, diagrams, pp. 5, 6-7, 14, 16-17; Doctor Stock / Getty Images, p. 8; Rob Marmion, p. 11; Roger McLean, pp. 18-19; Jose Luis Pelaez / Getty Images, pp. 20-21.